ORCHIDELIRIUM

2004

ORCHIDELIRIUM

DEBORAH LANDAU

2003 ANHINGA PRIZE FOR POETRY

Selected by Naomi Shihab Nye

ANHINGA PRESS, 2004
TALLAHASSEE, FLORIDA

Cover art: *Waiting Room I,* mixed media by D'vora Greenberg
Author photo: Marion Ettlinger
Cover design, book design, and production: C. L. Knight
Typesetting: titles set in Tiepolo; text set in Adobe Caslon

Library of Congress Cataloging-in-Publication Data
Orchidelirium by Deborah Landau – First Edition
ISBN 0938078-80-1 (paper)
Library of Congress Cataloging Card Number – 2004093500

This publication is sponsored in part by a grant from the Florida Department
of State, Division of Cultural Affairs, and the Florida Arts Council.

Anhinga Press Inc. is a nonprofit corporation dedicated wholly
to the publication and appreciation of fine poetry.

For personal orders, catalogs and information write to:
Anhinga Press
P.O. Box 10595
Tallahassee, Florida 32302
Web site: www.anhinga.org
E-mail: info@anhinga.org

Published in the United States
by Anhinga Press
Tallahassee, Florida
First Edition, 2004

for Mark,
and in memory of my mother

ACKNOWLEDGMENTS

Grateful acknowledgment is made to the editors of those
publications in which some of these poems first appeared: *The Antioch
Review, Barrow Street, Columbia: A Journal of Literature and Art,
Columbia Poetry Review, Crab Orchard Review, Grand Street, Gulf
Coast, Lyric Poetry Review, The Literary Review, Midwest Quarterly,
Mudfish, ONTHEBUS, Painted Bride Quarterly, Pool, Prairie Schooner,
Salamander, Spoon River Poetry Review,* and *Third Coast.*

"Lola and the Grape" and "Bathing" (Manhattan Fragment XI) were
anthologized in *Beyond the Valley of the Contemporary Poets.*

"Leave Taking" and "Lola and the Grape" (Part III) appeared in the
Los Angeles *Poetry in the Windows* festival.

My gratitude to all who helped usher this book into being, especially:
Kathryn Bowers, Patricia Carlin, Rick Campbell, David Dodd Lee,
Jessica Goodheart, D'vora Greenberg, Eve Grubin, Allan Jalon,
David Lehman, Daniel Lipschutz, Suzanne Lummis, Helen Kantor,
C. L. (Lynne) Knight, Mia Manzulli, Gretchen Mattox, Heather
McHugh, Kathleen Ossip, Molly Peacock, Davida Pines, Robert
Polito, Martha Rhodes, and David Trinidad. Much love and more
gratitude to my dear friend, Peter Nickowitz.

CONTENTS

ORCHIDELIRIUM

ONE

TO THE COUPLE LINGERING ON THE DOORSTEP

Quit kissing beneath my window.

The day turns shady
as you lean
feeding, feeding.

Night arrives, red-gold
and windless

and still you persist.

I've had enough
slobber and gush.

And let me say this:

the problem with passion
isn't that it doesn't last
but that it does,

and you'll find yourself alone in a room,
blistered and husky-voiced, watching
the side of your building turn to flame.

Beware a woman at a window,
something heavy in her hand.

HUMAN FRAILTY
(with help from Berlitz's *French for Travelers*)

I need a doctor
There's been an accident
I've got something in my eye

I've got a
blister
boil
bruise
burn
cut
graze
lump
rash
sting
swelling
wound

Could you have a look at it?

I'm not feeling well
I feel
dizzy
nauseous
shivery

I've got a fever
I'm vomiting
My _____ hurts

I have a vaginal infection
I have period pains
I'm pregnant

I have difficulties breathing
I have a pain in my chest
I've had a heart attack

Can you prescribe a/an
antidepressant
sedative
sleeping pill
painkiller
tranquilizer?

I don't want anything too strong

THE DISTANCE FROM
WHICH WE SEE OURSELVES

That sound in the room
means somebody's weeping.
Maybe it's me.

You could choke on this
and not go home.

Sometimes I confess to strangers,
sometimes I prefer not to speak.

Tonight, as you can see, it's foggy.
No moon but a muted smudge,

and I'm the woman at the payphone
asking the operator to repeat
those words I've never heard before.

I count the reasons to be unhappy;
line them up on the pillow, one, two, three,

leave the lights on into the night
to illuminate my darkness
until there's nothing left,

just a watery ache in my hands,
but I boil it until it's only vapor.

The sheets are cool and smooth,
in another world a metal door slams shut.

I move from room to room, looking for my mother
but find only a suitcase packed with shoes.

The nurse calls to say I've drowned,
but really I'm just resting in the water.

WINTER ON HUDSON STREET

I. Thanksgiving 1996

At the foot of this quilted red sofa
I hold the leg that troubles you.
We watch November close around the house.

Braced between your thickened limbs,
I rub your skin with Eucerin.
Mother, since summer,
the trees have lurched toward the drained pond.

I make no progress here.
Just when your flesh seems to soften
and my fingers seek the next ravaged spot
the muscle shuts again.

Your eyes laze left.
In the kitchen, that glazed bird
drools and nods.

Listen. Those Michigan crows
are calling everywhere in warning.
The oily sky slackens black.

God sits at our table
and hangs its head.

II. Sunday, West Village

Someone's left a window open over Bethune Street —
a typewriter clicks; from the radio mottled tunes, a weather forecast.

It's almost February but the guys on Seventh Avenue want to sell
me a Christmas tree from the curb with most of its needles missing,
one dollar each, better late than never.

When I get home the wide breath of afternoon empties itself
across my bed, where my boyfriend is still sleeping

and someone in apartment 312 is tuning a piano,
pressing the same key over and over,
until my dog cocks her head and listens, waiting for the note to open.

The oranges in my hands are from the Italian grocery on the corner
and make their own source of light, too bright in the stale air.

III. Columbia Presbyterian

On Monday my mother's oncologist offers
     only the incomprehensible.

I chew on his words like soft tar
     and spit them out.
They won't stay on the table
     won't stay in the toilet
won't stay in the bed pan.
     I try to swallow them
sour as turpentine.

All day I wear the sentence.
     I hit my head against it in the morning
and meet it again in the bathroom sink,
     midday I crash into it at the laundromat,
after dinner it lurks in my coffee cup.

At night I dream I carry a woman called Susan on my shoulders —
     balanced there, we pace a narrow platform.

IV. Nights, West Side Highway

Returning from the hospital late Tuesday by taxi,
the driver pulls a knife in the middle of Manhattan traffic,
peels a grapefruit, and offers me a slice.

On Wednesday, another driver wants to share his banana.
On Thursday, a bicyclist pulls up from behind,
asks if I'd like a stick of gum.

I think I'm losing my mind.

V. Rockaway Beach

Days, I teach in Brooklyn.

Standing in the classroom, legs cased safe in black cotton,
am I the same girl who came apart last night with every thrust?

This morning, one of my students rocks back in his chair,
thighs wide, a ring of silver round his neck —

from across the room I notice the shape of his groin,
shirt tucked tight against his belly, biceps curving beneath his sleeves.

Later, in the windowless office of the English department,
I open his journal, thick with script —

I was born in a small city in Ukraine,
there are many lakes and rivers in my motherland,
summer evenings, I'd walk in my grandmother's garden ...

the dark green ink of his pen.

VI. E-mail

Hi sweet,
how was your class?

What once was trivial becomes
something to be carefully kept;

her body diminishes, but her words
don't slur on the screen

and she can get around
just fine. All day long

my mother signals me.

VII. Self Exam

They say the princess
could feel a pea-sized lump
through twenty mattresses.

My breasts are more used-futon
than Serta-perfect, but every month
I prod their padding

barechested in my bed, so anxious
you'd think I was tied to train tracks.

I often look for the elusive —
out-of-print book, deep shade
of carmine lipstick, foreign
address of a man I once loved —
so this should be easy,

but looking for what you don't want
to find isn't looking, exactly —
more like a rush to rule out.

VIII. Snapshots

Leaving the theater one night
my mother felt for her broach —
found instead a pearl, seeded
in the shell beneath her clavicle.

In the photograph I keep,
she puts her face to the camera,
mild as summertime:

(the devil's farm blooming beneath her ribcage).

Each microscopic change takes years to matter —
meanwhile, I eat breakfast nine hundred times, sleep
with my boyfriend, grade papers, fret about the rent.

IX. Nights

In the kitchen, I'm alive in her nightgown at 3 a.m.
Each night, the clock reminds me.

I was there the moment she stopped breathing —
her whole body folding back,
blood purpling her neck like lace.

Three weeks ago I chose burial clothes,
fumbled among her shoes and necklaces
as the funeral man sat in her armchair
and took her dress and underwear.

I've woken for years to the same late stomachache
idling in the dark hallway between days
vague with smaller griefs.

But now this vivid, particular loss.

X. Nights

Her picture stares, sweet and simpler than she —
who never liked me grown careless and shaggy haired,
with bookshelves instead of a husband.

When she was sick I criticized her reticence
and could not stand to see her;

I've learned to love her better
since she left.

XI. Yartzeit

At Gristede's
I find the Yartzeit candle
between sponges
and mouse traps.

The clean white platform of wax,
stark as a hospital bed —
generic, stripped of particulars,
each loss is every loss.

After dinner, as its tiny fire
flutters in the glass
my niece sings *Happy Birthday*.

There's a prayer to chant,
but I don't know it.

Don't worry, my father says,

if anyone were listening,
we wouldn't need the candle.

XII. Washington Square Park

Downtown, we walk west on St. Mark's
past tables of incense and velvet hats and paperbacks,
that Japanese bar with the skinny black chairs, a florist
where hyacinths leak sweetness onto the sidewalk
and the amaryllis reverberate against all this gray —

and there's time to eat spanakopita at the Greek diner
across from the art house theater where for nine dollars
you can spend two hours in Paris with a box of junior mints,
and drink cappuccino from a paper cup.

Tonight, I'm free to walk through Washington Square
with a man I'm beginning to love as snow freshens the dog run
and women hurry home with bags of take-out salad bar
and the trees gesture darkly toward Waverly Place.

The gray buildings sharp against the sky.
The solid warmth of his hand through my fuzzed glove.

The hour is late but the shops don't close. The chill
from the sidewalk burns through my bootsoles,
and *mother* is a word I see in a bookstore window,
almost unreadable and far away.

LEAVE TAKING

The trees decide which way to go into winter.

One hems her narrow skirt scarlet.
One waits with a dog behind the white farmhouse.
One bends across an iron fence, yearning for another.
One sees her yellowed face in the mirror of a broken window.
One leans back to watch the dark stars blink out the day.

At the end of the street, the moon loosens his belt a notch.

LOLA AND THE GRAPE

I.

Animals can teach us things,
like, what to do with a gift you don't understand.

With persistence, my arthritic dog
learns to roll a grape between her paws —

the stray grape fallen
from the table cool and unfamiliar,

she settles in with her strenuous press,
waits for the yield.

II.

Eleven o'clock and I haven't even managed
to dress myself.

Beyond this window, the neighbor's boy
has placed his shining ladder in the sun.

The walls ripple with distraction
and I'm no longer alone, crunching dutch pretzels

to crumbs, the unremarkables of my life
hunched around like bored caribou

as the days move toward some stupid conclusion —
one I know and don't know

(what's come before, fixed and glittering
as a taxidermied peacock

and now only these gray beasts
trudging the shelves).

At least I can count on the dependable ants
to vacuum my mess with their grisly mouths —

narrow with purpose,
their steady marching.

III.

All day I watch the neighbor's boy
paint the side of his house.

He seems to rest so easily on the ladder rungs,
shirtless, lanky-limbed, hips tilting in the sun.

In the morning, I am the house, blueing beneath his brushstrokes,
each rib a shingle, my breasts, windowpanes, my waist,

the broad wood planks flattening beneath his brushstrokes,
my shoulders, shutters, lips and eyelashes fluttering eaves.

By four, I'm the roller brush,
turned and turning in his working hands.

Come dusk, I'm the open pail of paint
beside him on the grass — wide-mouthed, emptied.

The neighbor's house breathes in its new skin beneath the streetlamp.
It lifts its face to the darkness and does not recognize itself.

IV.

This room gone to pitch.
Only the screen's blue sheen.

Across the deepening lawn, the boy
collapses his ladder and disappears.

V.

And what if the chain of days
has turned smooth and bland as supermarket fruit?

Lola, on the carpet,
finds what's sweet is hidden.

What if, in this stillness,
in this creviced space between window

and chair, there's a sweetness,
ordinary as the present —

electric sun, blueglass of water, fur beside foot,
monitor hum, ants huddling crumbs,

the geometry of the body in its living skin,
its capacious hunger for evening,

for the nearness of another, clamoring
in darkness: *you are here, you are here* —

the steady, stubborn rise of human breath
along the trail from here to there.

TWO

DIVING LESSONS

She wants to fall, has practiced
letting her flesh pitch forward

chest packed flat in nylon, hair capped back,
sleek as a seal in her dark green Speedo.

She knows how to let the air claim her,
has seen the water waiting like a pale blue page

has watched the water blank as a bed sheet
has wanted the water wide as a young man's face.

She's memorized the trick of it —
the precise steps forward, snug spring,

measured lunge and funnel, pierced target
pooling quietly from the center in rings.

No one can reach her here, perched in the cool
of morning, text of the city rivering out below.

She arcs forward into the deep
air until she silvers through —

the heavy hush of water moving
like a skin on her skin —

then surfaces through ripples,
as a girl might slip from the body of her lover:

breathless, limbs glistening,
slick from touch.

SUNDAY AFTERNOON

As we slept I dreamt
we grew together
like two pale trees

stripped clean in late day light —
ankle to ankle; hip to hip,
the body having had its way,

needing nothing, equal among objects:
bookcase, bed frame, Japanese lamp,
lilacs sweet on the night table.

The potted palm moves its fingers,
your breathing deepens.
Slowly, the cats return,

the clock comes back into focus.
I lie still, watch its long hands
begin to move again above our bed.

THE EMPEROR'S CLOTHES

Even after you leave my bed,
long after midnight, muted
in black jeans and charcoal sweater —

as you walk home against the traffic on Second Avenue,
I know how your pale hips shift
when you step out to cross the street.

Even after you leave my bed, in lamplight,
firelight, and the bright air of Sunday afternoons,
I see your body —

more intricate than any costume,
more vivid than clocks or money,
better than the alphabet.

After you leave my bed, even then,
your legs unfold around me —
right thigh where the skin ripped once,

that jagged scar a seam,
skin of your rough knees,
suede patches on an old sweater,

soles of your feet darned thick
from the scrape of earth,
the wrinkly creases between your toes.

Even after, the embroidery of your palms
opens toward me in darkness
each finger tactile, separate;

I see your nipples, plum-colored buttons,
the whale bone corset of your ribs,
bolts of cloth pulled long, tight,

round the seamless cream of your waist,
cords of muscle like rope
tied snug and low over your hips,

that sleek dark stripe the path to your groin
where your sex curls in a skein of musky wool.
As you arc back against the headboard,

shiny beading above your mouth,
lips stained mauve and blackberry,
hemmed in jet filament

the silk of your eyelids;
unwrapped on the mattress,
your body ravels around me —

even after you leave.

ORCHIDELIRIUM

I.

Even in wedding white she feels obscene —
the chuppah laid in orchids, those flowers flaming,

and the guests fidgeting in their seats;
the women, labia seamed beneath them,

the men, polite in pressed trousers, the scent
shrouded in sprays and powders, wool and silk.

II.

A man brings a potted orchid to his wife.

Another Sunday.
She's peeling carrots and beets.

Orchids, she remembers, spring
from the spilled semen of mating animals —

those who succumb to the immodest blooms,
said to suffer from *orchidelirium*.

Bright juice stains the tile vermilion.
Strips of skin fall from her hands.

III.

Husband, beware your wife.

She hears the cellar door unlocking, shutters
sliding loose, the creaking foundation.

A radiator steams open an old box of letters —
clamor of the past, unsealing.

Wasn't this house rigged against motion,
a fermata hammered into every storm door?

No one's home. Only those decadent flowers
shuddering beneath their violet hoods.

The orchids taunt her, shake their cage,
take off their shirts and lift from their pots —

they've been breathing helium.
They know all about heat. Set loose,

flaming magenta, seething at the root.
Try to keep them here, they'll elude you,

leaving a gaudy trail of flares.

A PAIR OF MEN'S BRIEFS, SIZE 36

A pair of men's briefs, size 36,
neat and white as a chicken egg
appears in my laundry basket,

hatching havoc among my purples and blacks.
For two cycles they swam with my panties,
now stainless and bereft of musk

they nest with my nightie.
Whose genitals were stashed here?
What belly breathed against this waist band?

Newly monogamous, I realize
this is the closest I'll get to another man's crotch.
All week I inspect the guys in my elevator,

pray the briefs don't belong to the warty man
with the pipe, or the one in the leather cap
who mumbles "yeah, baby" in the lobby;

the boy with the Husky puppy, he'd be okay;
and I wouldn't mind the super either,
with his wispy hair and snug black t-shirt.

I'm keeping his underwear in my dresser for now,
they fit in nicely with my stockings and bras.
At night I dream they multiply, overflow my drawers

until the streets are filled with men who pace naked
beneath their jeans; while I, like Cinderella's prince,
size up each body, seeking a match.

FORGET WHAT THEY TOLD YOU

Uncross your legs
and leave the house
forget your mother
the veil
the wedding dress
let your mouth drop open
hang up the phone
allow all afternoon to fall around you
let it spin you forward
hold you up
as the seat reclines
unlock the grip on your coffee cup
let your shoes slip off
let the coins slide from your hands
forget your stop on the downtown train
discard the skillet
release the pearls
let the colors of honey
wash over you
when it comes for you
unfasten the moon
from its fragile case
and let it fly

MISCARRIAGE: FIVE ACTS

1)
Night is a red skirt spinning.
I busy myself with other things.

2)
I was expecting rain.
I was waiting for a kiss, but instead
found the janitor smoking
in my basement-crypt.

3)
And now, this grosbeak mobster
enters with rubbergloved hands.

My dear, he says, yours
is a scientific problem,
and I like you like this —
un-stockinged and clumsy.

4)
Throw another chokehold on my thicket,
Doctor, here are my leftovers,
half-baked and woozy.

Let me down easy, Mister Sloe Gin,
here is my collection of cut ups,
dead ends, clots, and X-ray.

See, I can make a summer Christmas
in emerald-green panties.

It's the Fourth of July, Labor Day,
it's goddamned Easter Sunday,
and I can't remember my name.

5)
The babies had been trying to get inside for years,
yanking my hems, scratching the backs of my calves,
so no wonder the first time I hiked my skirt
one got under.

The image crackled with static —
a child tossed from a swingset —

and then:
I'm alone again in my empty dress.

AFTER A TRIP TO THE FERTILITY CLINIC

The needle feeding at my arm
like a hummingbird,

doctors unlock
what I can't speak of

as I stray,
hollow as a wishing well.

At home,
that grandfather clock

wipes the air immaculate,
and even the books

have shut themselves
against further disturbance.

The walls shrink me
to the shape of my mother.

She will not forgive this.

False daughter, I'm dwarfed,
petty with emptiness,

and the heart's a sick house where I kneel
to undo her sharp hooks.

Am odd, misshapen.
There's nothing new to make.

MARITAL DISCORD

It might be something I said, might
not, but suddenly he's my father,

pressing down with the long thick hand
of his will — hook, jaw, and tenderspot —

and I'm thirteen, screaming
words I mean and don't

mean, until even the pillows shrink,
ashamed of their softness.

Beneath my wife suit
I'm raw and ugly as gooseflesh.

No sensation from the waist down, so cruel
I'm startled to catch sight of myself among the ruins.

Walls clawed with soot. The furniture
gone. I did this.

The roof splits open.
The room blues with cold.

BEARING DOWN

Listen
you said
moving
toward me
you
are reckless
and forgetful
I am tired
of your
body
and its
tedious
rhythms
your face
is an illness
I want
to forget.

After that
we got undressed.

I remember
eating
blueberries
from
a dark
purple
ceramic
bowl

the room clenched
with this new
poison.

BILLBOARDS AND OTHER SIGNS OF LOSS

I.

Because the Calvin Klein underwear man
hangs over West Hollywood

cocky as a weather vane,
I'm going to careen

across the median, smash
stationwagons, minivans,

as the asphalt sweats its dull mirage
and the erogenous buildings

shift and stiffen
in this late rise of heat.

From the dash, some aging radio therapist
laments "the appalling distraction

of sexual attraction." And look:
lounging above Sunset Boulevard

his gaudy flesh
huge as heaven.

II.

His hand never graces the back of my neck.

Strapped at the crosswalk
I check my blindspot

find no spirit there
but a man I'll never know

who stares and stares from the rented signboard
flashing his predictable come-ons.

And here I am, hands to the steering wheel,
making yet another left onto La Cienega.

And look at all the other souls
alone in their cars, braking toward home.

III.

Do you want to know your future?
The question awning the psychic storefront promises drama,

but I know my future will be as shoddy
as this street: hellish crush

of minimall and car wash, 7-Elevens
and six-dollar manicure shops.

The calendar suggests progress, but each week repeats.
Days, I tire of my own body; nights, I tire of yours.

When the sudden immediate heat of this stranger's face
sequined the gray of the usual, for a moment

I thought I knew what purpose was, what it would be to live
as though nothing were missing and nothing hurt.

I've wakened too many days in the same place,
turned in between the brows where I hold my mind shut,

exhausted, overfed, aching for any excuse
to feel good.

Only sign of God: this rapturous man above the traffic,
stupid with beauty.

TRAFFIC IN WEST HOLLYWOOD

It's late so I take off in the car's juicy accelerant,
swell and press of wheels, brakes tensed
as two of the best kind of lanky men pull in

to meet my glance, their truck darkened with windows.
And look, that one has his surfboard poking through
his sunroof like a huge goofy erection.

My body's just another piece of revved-up machinery
on these streets. Inconsolable, it wants what it wants.
Those boys, for instance, walking Sunset loose

in black pants, their bulldog huffing up against his stud collar.
Though even in dreams I can't go through with it, zipping up
at the last minute, frantic to fetch condoms or ask permission,

pulling back, only to wake beside a sleeping husband.
When I get to the café that boy behind the counter is smiling
with his blackberry lips as he handles my change,

rubbing the long bills between his fingers. He doesn't look up
but his mouth turns up. *Elvis rocks*, he says,
as the peach tea between us steams in its little glass mug.

Always this insistent music of want and want — don't speak all day,
but my eyes babble *kiss me* to the many that pass; thick calligraphy
of calf and ribcage, sidewalk flurry, untidy preliminaries.

Sick of the familiar clutch and slide,
the inherited, parental, marriage bed,
I crave what's strange:

those slanted hipbones, that face, his drinkable torso
jutting into my line of vision from the coffee shop window.
Want to tumble into the warped aperture

of back alley and empty lot, scatter and blaze.
But there's that same sun, polluting the parking lot.
And I'm strapped in again, heading home.

RAPUNZEL IN HOLLYWOOD

Rapunzel gets a haircut
at a West Hollywood salon.

I'm tired of being a ladder, she says
a man should find his own way up.

(In the tower, she slept without a boxspring,
tangled in her sheets while the feral cats
went at it all night in the garden,

her mother spoke in tongues
as she combed her into the oblivion
of lady-likeness,

and that prince, the smug fuck,
was a dead-end, pulling up in his Plymouth
to offer her a backseat life.)

The stylist turns on his blowdryer.
Her shorn hair fans out on the floor —
acres of it, useless.

There is space enough for a short-haired girl on Sunset Boulevard,
each open avenue gesturing westward toward the Pacific,
palm trees, strip malls, landslides, everything going down the long ride
off the edge of the continent —

she hitchhikes into the deep narcotic bliss of empty space
sends her mother a package from Venice —
a self-portrait from the photo-booth on the boardwalk,

I'm living a fine dream
unlearning the weight of your fingers

her ponytail coiled inside like a snake.

DUSK ON MULHOLLAND DRIVE

1. Each Year I Grow Smaller

Each year I grow smaller,
shed selves like those Russian dolls
hardening into the singular
glazed mannequin
wife.

Dusk on Mulholland Drive,
fire roads spike into the burntbrown hills
and I'm winding home along the spine of the city
as the thousand thousand lights click on
Ventura Boulevard strung out below like a fractured bone —

this city is fat with gas stations and tract homes,
where someone's shaking a tablecloth, scraping dishes,
clipping a child's moony fingernails,
where a radio's on so the dog won't be lonely,
where couples sleep, wrapped in the marriage bed,
that thick gauze bandage.

Once evening was a clear glass bowl
empty of everything.

Once I was sixteen girls
in sixteen cities,
all of them possible.

2. Making Friends (with help from Berlitz's *French for Travelers*)
(Comment se faire des amis)

Do you mind if I sit here?
Can I get you a drink?
Are you free this evening?
Why are you laughing?
Is my French that bad?
Would you like to go dancing?
Shall we go to the cinema?
Shall we go for a drive?
I'll pick you up at your hotel.
Thank you, it's been a wonderful evening.
May I take you home?
Can I see you again tomorrow?

3. Work

In line at the campus café, my student,
taller than I'd realized, leans in from behind —
his beat-up leather jacket brushing the back of my neck.

Later, he sits in the front row of my classroom, points
to a sexual reference in *Song of Myself* I'd somehow missed.

I imagine the bulk of him undressed — sudden rush,
the body interrupting to say, *I'm here.*

After class, distracted,
I walk into the men's room.

4. Evening Commute

It's dark. The Santa Ana winds are sweeping the canyon.
The season's turning back upon itself
and I am tired of restless heat.

There's a postcard on the dashboard —

quai st michel, rue saint jacques ...

there are streets that lead out of here.

5. Home

But when I get home
he's in the green armchair in the corner reading,

his forehead a complex map, his gaze
fixed on the page, sharp and exacting,
that watch we bought together years ago.

There's a look on his face he doesn't wear with me
and I feel like I'm cruising a stranger
admiring the slope of his shoulders,
the smooth flesh on the side of his neck.

All day I've flirted with another kind of life
then circled back to look so closely
he's become strange again as any man —

the way you say the same word over and over
until it changes, becomes unbound sound
set loose from its bedded groove.

Do you mind if I sit here?
Are you free this evening?
May I take you home?

He doesn't see me so doesn't look up
but stays, cupping his book
in the circle of light from the standing lamp.

THE OPPOSITE OF SUFFERING IS SPACE

All night jackhammers stammer beneath the window.
The man lying beside me exhales, says, *it's late*, turns away.

This mattress is a cave, a bit deeper every night,
where we've hurried again, fitful for the usual
push into pleasure, the buckling over,
the predictable, tawdry arrival.

Notice the doughy torso, smoothed of grooves,
the freakish bleached hipbones,
collapsible ribs, drab library of arms
and feet.

All night, beneath the window,
the streets open and close their cracked hands.

As if our pairing could spawn what is wished for,
we keep returning to the same strained place.

Listen. Even the sky
is absent here. Ask for the ocean
and only the earth beats down.

FROM NEVADA, IN DEFENSE OF MY MARRIAGE

*Love does not make itself felt in the desire for copulation but in
the desire for shared sleep ...*
            — Milan Kundera, *The Unbearable Lightness of Being*

Sunday morning, Laughlin. Heat damns us poolside.
All week we've been trying to shed the marriage bed.

Remember how desire wasn't lilac-petaled?
It was heavy. It swaggered, gave commands,

could make us lie down
in heat in the middle of a workday.

On the empty deck I squint at the *Times* —
the newspaper's muted violence unfolding in my lap —

while Angie, ex-Vegas waitress in crucifix earrings
and velvet halter-top, speaks to you of Jesus.

When we drove out of L.A., dust warping the windows
of our rented blue Lumina, is this what we were looking for —

this $39 motel room, broken church where we worship
the miracle of too many margaritas and pay-per-view porn?

Later, when I wake to the radio testing the Emergency Broadcast System
you're sleeping beside me in the sapphire light of the clock's crystal

digits, veins braceleting your wrists, powerlines
surging toward the circuit of your wedding ring —

sometimes my restlessness syncopates the day's anatomy
and all I want is to slouch in the darkest bar on the other side

of the continent, numb with wine, dissolving between the borders
of midnight and 4 a.m., a stranger's face leaning toward me …

but look, the message light's blinking through the tequila bottle,
tilted amber hourglass, your breath has emptied itself against my breasts,

and we're still here amidst the wreckage of flesh —
t-shirt, sandal, minidress, curtains hushing the sun.

We've got hours until check-out. Maybe the door's jimmied
but the chain still holds, and for now I'll take this communion:

your volatile mouth, long scar cracking your chest, anchor
of your face stained with our history, your crucial, exact glance.

THREE

AIR TRAVEL

Anxiety rings like a payphone in an empty booth —
hard glint of moon on knifebladewings,
the yanked-tooth skyline
and tiny reading lights of Manhattan. I'm pleading
with the beverage cart for something to stop this insistent noise.

I'm either thinking about death,
or, thinking about death, often both at the same time.
I've got a mouthful of Juicyfruit, grabbag of Xanax,
I come out of the lavatory with toilet paper stuck to my shoe.
Night comes on sudden and empty as the airsickness bag in front of me.

Understand, the traytable locks must be vertical, *vertical*,
when you weren't looking I straightened yours,
and you should thank me, they make the plane fly straight,
without me it wouldn't even get off the ground.

I pat the plane's silver skin on boarding
good plane nice plane so masculine capable tough.

~

The cockpit breaks off
and you continue to travel forward
awash in the cold night air.

You realize you are a rootless soul.
You grow impatient on the lavatory line.
You are not Icarus. You like to stay on the ground.
You'd like your parachute
but it's stowed in the overhead bin.

The man beside you has shaved his body.
The girl beside you takes your picture without asking.
The wind blows in through the exit door.

The flight attendants pantomime grimly.
There is no chance of rescue.
The seatcushions are filled with sand
and the lifejackets, though useless,
are an appealingly vivid shade of lemon yellow.

~

The plane does not exist.
The plane is a metaphor.
The plane is a bird winging south in a straight straight line
glimpsed by a nervous girl
lying on the school gymnasium floor.

It communicates with sophisticated clicks.
It says, soon you will arrive in Cleveland.

The plane is a dream of bees, a disc of moon,
the first new being of an alien race.

The plane is a tired bird now,
looking for a sleeping space.

The gymnast tugs her shoe,
flexes her foot over her head into the air.

She considers her attachment to the ground,
her solitary body fastened beneath the transparent blue
where all borders give way to emptiness.

She leans back and plucks the plane out of the sky.
She punts it into the rafters. She makes it disappear.

Then silence. No more booms or twittering.
The end, for the moment, of the jitters.
The night janitor comes on to mop up.

MANHATTAN FRAGMENTS
(2001-2002)

I.

No use for beds.
No use for cradles,
quilts, the sky blue
rocking chair.

No use for the rug,
there on the hearth,
or the hearth,
made for warming.

I finger the *Times*
A hard coin where my heart used to be, flipping.

II.

Candles.
Letters.
The empty shell of a shoe.

When the wind shifts

she walks toward me
paper-masked
little chip of winter
blue handed and not alive

when the wind shifts
each loss is every loss.

She brought a snow colored orchid
brief wisp

the next day she was —

(the orchid flowering on dispassionately)
a blank space

what's not here is —
palpable absence
here

when the wind shifts,

the hand reaches for the phone
to (re)call her

the eye looks southward
expecting something solid in the sky

the mind keeps firing
along these phantom limbs

III.

And so, the body is exhausted
and couldn't possibly make love.

Stalled in darkness
deep beneath midtown

a narrowing in the tube

backdrop
comes into focus

Korean man sleeping
nervous woman in a skirt

my own pale oval
reflected back at me from across the car

PRAY
graffitied on the tunnel wall.

It came and will come again.

The unfamiliar words on the tongue
felt foreign at first then clicked
against the dry roof hard, like rain.

Ten months since I'd taken a good deep breath.

IV.

You must leave everything behind,
your body of water, your stream of breath,
something static in your hand like a wing.

It came and will come again:
flooding Fifth Avenue through Washington Square
and the strong swimmers will shed their day clothes
and climb into the fountains
and the ticketholders will find themselves unlucky
and the desk clerks will wave their flags
and the scaffolding will collapse
and the morning light will come down hard
on the sidewalk, nothing to break its fall.

V.

Since there will be no more love
I take the arm of a man I don't know
while the sky greens key lime
as a formica counter in a 24-hour diner

where a priest is finishing a pie in the corner,
eating himself alive, hoping no one will notice,
and a couple has put down their coffee cups
and walked out together into the empty parking lot.

Tonight, in a crisis of faith
I wander from block to block, hoping to forget,

but every radio in this city blares the same song,
an ambulance racing
and I'm just whistling along in synch —

how to proceed
with our insect lives, working the trail,
or burrowing underground.

VI.

It must be a solitary woman who says, winter,
who says, gather those pine needles failing the trees,
the wealth of snow, the sky greying my hair, creasing my cheeks.

If the snow could speak it would tell me where you are,
the winter light dimming and me unsuited for storm,
shivering along Fifth Street.

All day the buses ride the avenues without you.
Here, in the thin slice of light
splicing Houston Street

your absence stalls me —
spruce tree on the curb,
pestle of boots on sidewalk mortar —

What does the snow know about comings and goings?
You've not gone far, I say, flute from an open window,
curtains fraying against firmament, unwatered fern.

VII.

The city empties and fills again
a premature and vivid spring,
steroidal flowers —

January daffodils in Gramercy Park,
Magnolia blossoms in Washington Square
fat, brown, burnt out.

The air here comes in every shade of yellow.

My neighbor's newborn
finds home in lower Manhattan —

his muffled smell, his fragile neck,
blanketed in baby blue

as if the center of the world were tender.

Morning on Crosby Street.
Flattened rat on the cobblestone —
irresistible to my dog,
who's faithful only to her appetites,
thinks death's delicious, wants to lick it up.

VIII.

In March
more birds

appeared in the sky
long dark wings

tipping the horizon
like aircraft

suspicious
because everything was

even the most natural thing
startled, caused flight.

IX.

Slowly I relearn this city, block by block —

first warm storm on Mercer Street
where we loved a German film one winter

red rainstreaked sign, FANELLI CAFÉ

lifesized pink panther doll
atop the dumpster.

(What is lucid?

was there soul-ejection?

hover
                in the in-between

some just emerging others just?)

X.

How mournful the watertowers are, squatting
on the rooftops in their wiry corsets,
their slate-colored despair —

maybe I could learn something from them about containment,
the virtue of holding still.

Trick of perspective: I could tip
them over with a flick of my finger,
flooding streets, buildings, setting loose
one hushed rush — everything
free-floating down Broadway toward the harbor.

XI.

The dead haven't left.

Even the walls of this room,
the futon and telephone —
thick with residue.

When the streets quiet
I feel the brush

of my mother's long hair, scent
of lemon balm —

years later,
what's not here

is here.

XII.

In the late day light
I wash your hair.

Outside the window
Grand Street happens all afternoon.

You float in the water between my legs
I bathe your face, your throat, your hands;

when I inhale
your chest rises.

Begins with bed
and ends in water —

lips, thighs, and shoulders
set loose from the city at four o'clock.

The day unravels.
This space ripples, shimmers, and is still.

In the rising steam
your skin is shining,

the taste of your body
is in these words,

I could live for ages
eating from this luminous table.

XIII.

And we find ourselves wobbly
in our new loose-fitting skins.

Even in bed, we are relearning the lingo,
everything slightly askew, too fragile to take for granted.

All night, we turn toward each other, then away —
the ruckus of trucks
the manifold sirens, and something else,
the curtains, the clock, the shatter of wind,
and our own breathing, unmoored and swept along.

ABOUT THE AUTHOR

Deborah Landau was born in Colorado and grew up in Ann Arbor, Michigan. She was educated at Stanford, Columbia, and Brown, where she was a Javits Fellow and earned a Ph.D. in English and American Literature.

Her poems have appeared in numerous literary magazines, including *Columbia, Grand Street, Barrow Street, The Antioch Review,* and *Prairie Schooner,* and she has published critical articles on contemporary American poetry. She was a two-time winner of the Los Angeles Poetry in the Windows Contest, a National Poetry Series finalist and was nominated for a Pushcart Prize.

Landau has taught at Brown, Antioch, and NYU, and is currently a core faculty member and Assistant Chair of the Writing Program at The New School. She is co-curator of the *KGB Poetry Reading Series* and lives in New York City.

THE ANHINGA PRIZE
FOR POETRY SERIES

**Out of print*